T0146548

LET'S
WORK
—— *with* ——
LEATHER

DELFIN ESTANISLAO

authorHOUSE®

AuthorHouse™
1663 Liberty Drive
Bloomington, IN 47403
www.authorhouse.com
Phone: 1 (800) 839-8640

© 2017 Delfin Estanislao. All rights reserved.

No part of this book may be reproduced, stored in a retrieval system, or transmitted by any means without the written permission of the author.

Published by AuthorHouse 04/05/2017

ISBN: 978-1-5246-6909-6 (sc)
ISBN: 978-1-5246-6907-2 (hc)
ISBN: 978-1-5246-6908-9 (e)

Library of Congress Control Number: 2017901120

Print information available on the last page.

Any people depicted in stock imagery provided by Thinkstock are models, and such images are being used for illustrative purposes only.
Certain stock imagery © Thinkstock.

This book is printed on acid-free paper.

Because of the dynamic nature of the Internet, any web addresses or links contained in this book may have changed since publication and may no longer be valid. The views expressed in this work are solely those of the author and do not necessarily reflect the views of the publisher, and the publisher hereby disclaims any responsibility for them.

CONTENTS

PREFACE

Working with leather has always been satisfying and profitable. Just by looking around and watching how women buy and use their handbags, and men their wallets and belts, we can surmise that this old, old raw material has been tested by time as a good source of pride and of income.

However, despite the satisfaction gained in working with leather and the profit that can be generated once the item being made has been multiplied and sold for the enjoyment of others, people from developing countries can not copy or make same things found in the market because of lack of knowledge and skills that will help them work with leather the same way a cabinet maker or carpenter makes things from wood. Hence, the opportunity for work of the individual as an employee or as a self-employed is lost. Students who can be trained in early age to gain skills specially in working with leather have been left unaided, therefore opportunity is gone both for the individual and eventually for the country. It is in this premise that this book is written: To encourage and gain the basic skills that are used in making things from leather. The projects incorporated in this book which can be used for practice to gain skills are believed will be of help to the beginner. The projects are arranged from the simplest to the most complicated ones with the hope of motivating the reader, the prospective leather goods maker, who eventually can be a self- employed individual. Likewise, information about the different categories of leather goods and how they are sold according to season will hopefully help future exporters to the industrialized countries. Last, but not the least, is a project on how to make a men's sandal without using a wooden last, which again is hoped to spark interest in shoe making.

Since this is the first attempt of the author to spark interest in this field, the reader is encourage to give comments and suggestion in order to make this book a good reference material.

The author acknowledges and gives thanks to the Author of Life, our Almighty Father for giving him the opportunity to be of service to those who will benefit from this book.

History of Leather

Leather which is the processed covering of animals has been a popular raw material in making items used in our daily living even before the birth of Christ. Quotation from the book of St. Mathew, c.9 v17 states:" people do not pour new wine into old wineskin. If they do, the skin burst, the wine spills out and the skin is ruined. No, they pour new wine into the new wineskin and in that way both are preserved ".

From here we can affirmed that the used of leather has been popular even before the birth of Christ. Some ancient records said that the used of leather has been popularized by the Romans and Hebrews. At one time, the Romans used leather as a basis as well as making helmets, shields and sandals. The materials used in whipping Jesus was said be made from leather. Some historians claimed that the Hebrews used the sap of the Oak tree as to a curing agent to turn the skin of animals into leather. Among the early uses of leather during the ancient times were cover for the bookbinder items, scrolls and parchments. One of the finest leather during that time was Morocco, which was made from the skin of lambs and goats.

In the orient, the Chinese were credited for using salt and Alum mixed with mud in curing the skin of animals. Some history books say that when Marco Polo was visiting India, he found that the bed covers in this country were already made of leather and even dyed with red and blue colors.

The Moors and the Spaniards used leather extensively for making saddles and harnesses. Those articles were beautifully decorated with designs and jewels. In Cordova, the leather center of Spain, Cordovan leather was developed from horse hide.

At the other part of world, the American Indians learned that by wearing leather moccasins they could run faster specially during their hunting period. These natives also discovered that the hide of the buffaloes could make sturdy and weather proof tents Using leather as a string they could lace the heavy stone in a stick or branch of a tree to be used as a tomahawk. To make a buckskin, the American Indians soaked the skin in a lye solution made from wood ashes, scrapped off the hair and flesh and then dried over a teepee for several days.

` Today, the leading brands that produce fine leather handbags, shoes and other leather goods are Coach, Louis Vitton, Salvatore Ferrigamo, Gucci, Furla, Hermes and others. This means that until today, there is nothing like working and using leather.

TANNING PROCESS

The process by which the skin of animals is converted into leather is tanning. After the animal has been killed, the skin is quickly separated from the flesh then cured. What follows then is a series of work involving the use of chemicals in order to make the material suitable for what it is intended. During the tanning process, steps like eliminating the odor to make the smell tolerable while being worked on, removing the hair on the skin, making the surface more smooth, soft and pliable, and dyeing to have the needed color for the item or project to be made are done.

Tanning is a different field of study. The process mentioned above was given only to make the leather worker understand how this material is made. The person who makes leather is called a tanner.

KINDS OF TANNING

1) Chrome Tanning - is the process of making leather by using chemicals. The leather used in making shoes are made from this process.

2) Vegetable Tanning - is the process making leather using the sap of the bark of a tree or any natural material. Tooling leather which you will use is made from this process.

3) Combination Chrome and Vegetable – is the process of using both chemical and sap of wood or any natural material in making of leather. Some special kinds of shoes are made from this material.

SOURCES OF LEATHER

There are three different technical terms used to define where leather comes from.

1) Skin - refers to the leather taken from small animals such as snake, goat, lamb, sheep and lizard.

2) Hide - refers to the leather taken from big animals such as cows, buffaloes, alligators and other animals that weigh more than 80 pounds.

3) Kips - are leather taken from the young of large animals that weigh from 15 to 30 pounds.

BUYING LEATHER

Leather is sold by weight or in some instances by square foot (sq. ft.). Below is the chart.

Ounces	Iron	Fraction Inches	Decimal Inches	Metric
1 oz.	.75	1/64	0.016	0.41mm
2 oz.	1.50	1/32	0.081	0.78
3 oz.	2.25	1/64	0.047	1.19
4 oz.	3.00	1/16	0.063	1.60
5 oz.	3.75	5/64	0.078	1.98
6 oz.	4.50	3/32	0.094	1.39
7 oz.	5.25	7/64	0.109	2.78
8 oz.	6.00	1/8	0.125	3.18
9 oz.	6.75	9/64	0.141	3.58

10 oz	7.50	5/32	0.136	3.96
11 oz.	8.25	11/64	0.172	4.37
12 oz	9.00	3/16	0.188	4.78
13 oz	9.75	13/64	0.203	5.17
14 oz.	10.50	7/32	0.219	5.57
15 oz.	11.25	15/64	0.234	.95

CRAFT LEATHER

In making articles from leather including shoes and clothing, the maker should know which side of the leather should be used. The crafter should use the side where the hair grows. It should be noted, however, that since the skin has already been processed the hair has already been shaved. In the industry his is called the **grain side** or simply **full grain**. This side has a smooth finished surface and has a compact fiber that makes the surface wear well. Underneath the grain is technically called **flesh side**. This part of leather has a rough surface because this part is the one that is attached to the flesh before the animal is killed.

The other type of leather is called **split leather.** Split leather is made by dividing the thickness of the leather into two parts. The top part which is smooth will be embossed and the other part or side will be made to appear smooth but this layer is less firm.

TYPES OF LEATHER

A) Full Grain Side leather – This type of leather is obtainable in a variety of color natural being the most popular. If you will be using the calf skin, this leather measures 9 to 12 Sq. ft. and weight from 1 ½ to 3 1/3 oz. per square foot. Mostly made by using either the vegetable or chrome tanning method, this leather has a smooth satins like finish and usually uniform in weight and wears extensively well. However, calf skin is a soft and requires stiffener when used in big projects making shoes. Full grain, if vegetable tanned is the one used for tooling and curving. On the other hand, full grain chrome tanned side is good for making purses, handbags, belts, whether for men or women, shoes, sandals and other leather goods item which do not require tooling or curving design.

B) Cow Hide –Cow hide is heavier than calf skin because cow is the parent and calf is the offspring. Cow hide does not have a smooth satin like finish.

It is usually purchased in a term called **side**. A **side** measures about 22 to 24 sq. ft. Whole hide will certainly be too large to handle. A sq. ft. of cow hide weighs from 4 to 16 oz., therefore, if you plan to buy this kind of leather, specify whether you want 4-5 oz. or 9-10 oz. leather.

C) Sheep Skin - Taken from the skin of the sheep, this leather is soft, porous and does not have the shine or luster of the calf skin. This leather can not withstand wear and should not be used that are subject to strenuous wear. Sheep skin is excellent in making small projects suited for beginners in projects. This leather is also excellent as lining for bigger articles. Sheep skin leather used in tooling usually comes in natural color and is 7 to 10 sq. ft. size and weighs 1 ½ to 3 oz. per sq. ft. When ordering, specify the color and weight.

D) Morocco and Goat Skin - Morocco is usually hard grain with a very rich texture and is sold in a variety of colors. This kind of leather is largely used for handbag linings or pockets of billfold wallets. This leather is used in tooling. Meantime, goat skin is usually about 6 sq. ft. in size and the width ranges from 2 to 2 ½ oz. per sq. ft.

E) Pig Skin - The grain of this leather has a distinct appearance. The surface is divided into triangular areas made by lines of hair follicles from one place to the other. The skin measures 6 to 7 sq. ft. and is available in natural tones as well as other colors. The weight is about 2 ½ oz. per sq. ft. Used for tooling, this leather is inexpensive hence good for beginners. If not used as tooling leather, the skin is an excellent material for lining in shoes.

NON TOOLING LEATHER

Below is a list of different kinds of leather which are not suitable for tooling or carving. However, they can be used in making any other kind of project, big or small, in order to show its own natural surface design.

A) Alligator grain calf - The grain side of calf skin was embossed to resemble the natural design of the genuine alligator skin. This leather is sold in many different colors and usually comes in 8 to 10 sq. ft. and is about 2 ½ oz. in width.

B) Lizard grain calf - The design of the genuine ground lizard is embossed in the side of the leather. It is usually available in black and brown, 8 to 10 sq. ft., and weighs about 2 ½ oz. per sq.

C) Snake Skin - This kind of leather taken from the covering of snake is thin but strong. This leather is suitable for ladies shoes, belts and handbags. Available in a variety of colors, and is 9 in. at the widest part and averages about 4 to 5 ft. in length. It is sold by piece.

D) Ostrich - Ostrich is the common bird skin used for leather. It has a luxurious appearance and will wear well. This can be used for wallets, coin purses, handbags, and ladies shoes. The leather is expensive. In case you are interested in using this, just buy enough for your particular project.

LINING LEATHERS

The following leathers are used in coin purses, billfolds, key containers, key holders and Pigskin other similar projects or items which require lining. These leathers do not have enough body to stand as exterior for any leather goods.

A) Pig skin – Pigskin is used mainly for gloves and frequently for lining in wallets and purses or ladies handbag. This is obtainable in different colors. The skin usually weighs about 2 oz. per sq. ft. and measures 6 to 8 ft.

B) Suede Garment (Sheep Skin) - This particular leather has a fine surface and is very supple. Also available in a variety of colors, the size and weight correspond to that of a sheep.

C) Skiver - A skiver is the grain split of a sheep skin. This is used to line handbags, and purses, to bind books and to make hat bands. Skivers are economical and easy to obtain.

D) Crushed or Ecrace Goat Skin - Ecrase is a French word that means crushed. Crushed leather has the natural or artificial grain accentuated by plating. Some other processed may have been used to preserve the outline of the grain or design. The design makes the leather superior material for lining. It averages about 2 oz. per sq. ft. and is available in several colors.

PARTS OF LEATHER

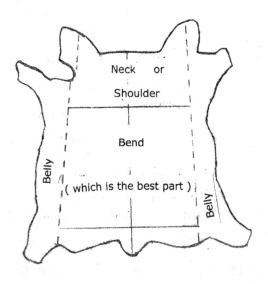

Fig. I Parts of Leather

Tools Used In Carving And Tooling

Considering the variety of things or items that we can make with leather, it is interesting to know that only a few tools are required.

For surface design 1) **Tooling or stamping technique** – This is the process of making of impression on the surface of a tooling leather while the surface of the leather is damp. Sometimes this technique is also called stamping. To begin with this technique, all you need are the stamping tools and mallet or hide hammer.

2) **Modeling** - This is done by making incision or pressing the line of a design on the surface of the leather using a modeler (see picture) and a swivel knife. A *modeler* has a flat spoon-shaped head on one end and a smooth pointed stylus on the other. A swivel knife is used to carve lines on the tooling leather. That is why making lines and drawings on leather is sometimes called "carving".

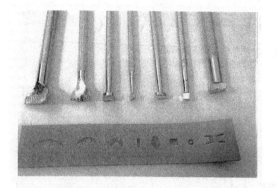
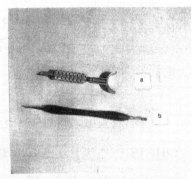

Fig. 2 - Tools used in Stamping and Modeling – 1) Stamping Tools (basic) with impression 2) Modeling Tools (a)-swivel knife (b) modeler (c) Alphabet stamping set (d) Types of Modelers

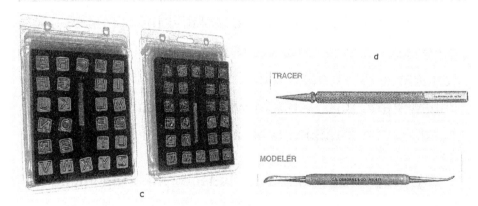

The best for all around tooling work. One end is narrow and pointed, suitable for line work or tracing, the other end is flattened, suitable for any type of modeling.

14

OTHER TOOLS TO BE USED

A) Cutting Tools

1) Knife -is mainly used to cut leather. For thick leather that weighs 7 oz. or more, a cobbler's knife (sometimes called shoemaker's knife) is used for cutting and separating pieces of projects that have thicker parts. At times, this knife can be used in reducing the thickness of any kind of leather. However, here are the other types of knives used for different purposes:

   A) Round Head Knife - The blade forms half moon; recommended for cutting heavy leather.

   B) Bevel Point Knife - used for skiving or slicing away leather at a point where its too thick; also used for trimming edges.

C) Skiving Knife - as the term implies, used to reduce the thickness of leather. This piece of knife is much smaller than the round head.

D) Skife Knife - also used in reducing the thickness of the leather; the blade of the skife is replaceable by injecting the blade. The idea is for the knife not gouge the leather too deeply.

E) Cutter or Cutting Knife - the blade can be shaped on a 60 to 90 degrees angle to make it look like the back of a parrot. There is a round handle at the end of the knife.

2) Cutting Board – This could be a piece of plywood or the commercial thick rectangular plastic board used to protect the surface of your working table. A piece of flat aluminum is also good as a cutting board since the surface of this metal is smooth and make the cutting of pieces smoother.

3) Leather scissors or leather shears – There are two types of scissors that are used in leather craft. The first one has a serrated blade and the other is a plain scissor with a longer blade. For

some light works, however, cutting knife will give a straight cut on the edges of the leather.

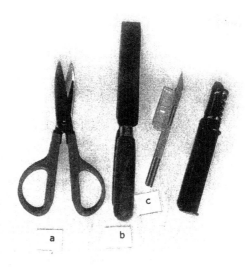

Fig. 3 – Cutting Knives (a) scissors (b) Skiving knife (c) Cutting knife

B) Measuring Tools

Metal Square/Steel Square and Steel Rule – There will be instances that a steel rule or metal square will be used in cutting straight edges.

Dividers – Used in making marks to guide distances of holes where laces and/or stitches will be placed.

C) Punchers

Manual or Drive Punchers – called either manual or drive punchers because a mallet or hard wood is used to drive them to make holes for snaps, rivets, grommets. In some cases, specially designed punchers are used for decorative purposes.

D) Mallet or straight 1 ½" x 2" hard wood – used to drive punchers.

E) Shoe Hammer – A light weight hammer to press the edges of a project to make the bonding stronger.

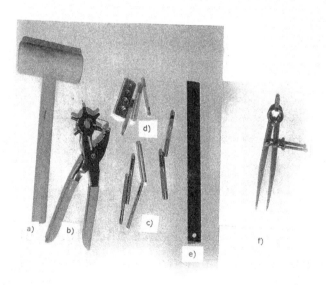

Fig. 4 – Measuring and Punching Tools – (a) Mallet (b) Rotary Puncher (c) Hand held Puncher (d) Setter (e) Ruler (f) Divider (g)Shoe Hammer (h) Leather Goods working hammer (I) Scratch Awl

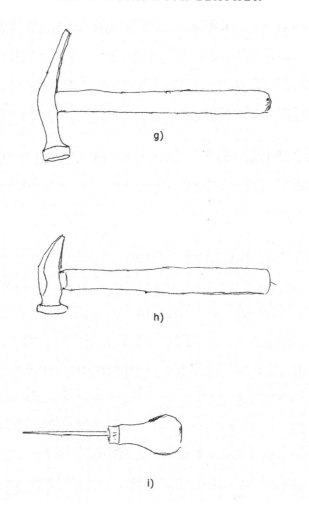

g)

h)

i)

F) Stitching or Sewing Tools

As soon as the holes for stitching or lacing have been punched, you are now ready to assemble the projects either by sewing, stitching or lacing. Remember, the evenly punched holes give a professional look.

1) **Harness Needle** – a long sturdy needle with an egg-shaped eye with a dull point. Used for

stitching with a wax thread through the pre-punched holes. This needle is available in different sizes. Triple zero (000) is good for any purpose. The hole is approximately 2 ½" long.

2) **Stitching Awl** – This tool gives the same lock stitch effect like the sewing machine. Used mainly for heavy leather.

3) **Sewing machine** – There are 2 types of sewing machines for this particular area of work. The *flat bed* which is the same or similar to that of the machine used by a tailor or the dressmaker. Only the presser foot is used for thicker leather or canvass. The second type is the *cylinder type.* This is used by the shoemakers in making the upper part of the shoe. There are other type of special machine for leather craft but I only mentioned this so the beginner won't be confused. Later, when the leather crafter becomes more acquainted with the trade, he or she would know other types of machine to use.

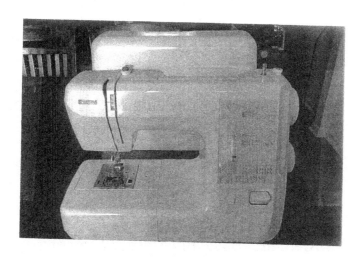

Fig. 5 – (a) Stitching Awl (b) Sewing Machine

Special Tools

Snap Setter - used in putting snaps

Grommet - A two piece tool consisting a tube-like round piece with a hole at the base. This tool has numbers for identification purposes. No. 2 zero is the most common.

Eyelet Setter- Used to fasten eyelet on belt, vests or any part of the project that will protect the holes from wear and tear. In lieu of an eyelet setter, the beginner can use a 2 or 3 common nail to fasten the "legs" of the eyelets.

Stud Setter - Used for a number of jobs. This tool has an adaptor to enable the set of studs stay fixed at the surface of the leather.

Scratch Awl – used for piercing or marking leather.

SUPPLIES NEEDED

Rubber Cement - Basically, rubber cement is used to join or bond the different pieces of the project together whether joining or assembling the different pieces temporarily or permanently. The leather crafter must know in advance what type of rubber cement to use. The store owner can give the maker an advice on this. Again, bear in mind that rubber cement can either be used for permanent bonding or temporary adhesion.

Sewing Thread - Sewing thread can either be polyester or cotton. The thread used in making leather craft projects has a heavier count. The store owner can guide you which thread is best for smaller projects and for heavy project.

Stains and Dyes - Used in making the items or projects colorful.

Rivets - Used to join smaller parts of the project that involves decoration. Since this is chrome coated, joining pieces together with rivets makes the project get its unique presentation. Rivets always comes in pairs.

Sponges, Paint Brush and Rubber Gloves.

Bees Wax Cake - Use in making the heavy thread water proof.

OTHER SUPPLIES USED ON A CASE TO CASE BASIS

1) Buckles 2) Snaps (sometimes called claps) 3) Decorative hole punchers 4) Metal hinges and Lock 5) Buttons 6) Nail Heads and Studs

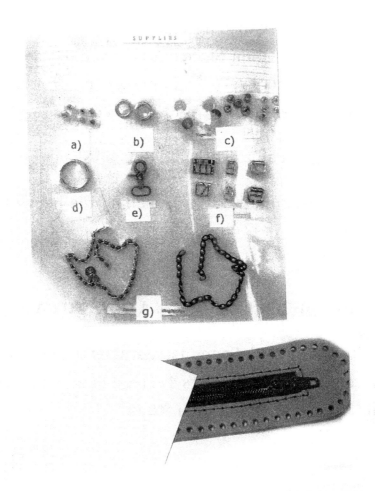

Fig. 6 – Accessories sometimes called supplies

a) rivets – has different sizes   b) eyelets – has different sizes   c) snaps – has a magnetic type and non magnetic type   d) ring – has different diameters   e) strap holder – has various models   f) buckles – has different models or designs   g) zipper – comes in different sizes and colors to blend on the materials used.

TECHNIQUES OR SKILLS IN MAKING PROJECTS

At the outset, the author believes that no amount of words can describe the different techniques or skills in making projects better than illustrations or drawings and/or hands on. In this regard, the author made every effort to describe a technique and whenever possible provided illustrations to make the transfer of skill more practical and rewarding. Likewise, projects included in this book were arranged from the easiest to complicated ones to make the beginner feel more assured or confident in learning a certain technique.

A) ***Laying down or transferring the pattern*** – The patterns accompanying the different projects on this book can be copied or traced. Once the pattern is copied or made, it is ready to transfer that to the leather. To transfer the pattern, lay it down on the true side of the leather. With a pencil or tracer, trace the whole outline. Please note on thinner leather i.e., 1 oz. to 5 oz, pencil can be used. But for more than 5 oz. a scratch awl or tracer should be used. TAKE NOTE: 1) Always use a ruler or steel square to aid in tracing a straight line. 2) If you are working on a big project, you can raise one end of the design occasionally to find out if the leather you are working on is taking the clear impression of the design and no lines have been missed. 3) If you have a steady hand and would like to have a professional look of the design, the small end of the modeler which is called stylus is used for tracing the design. 4) Never use a carbon paper in tracing the design.

B) **Cutting leather** - This process requires that you already have copied or transferred the pattern and the number the number of parts to be cut. You need a sharp knife and a good cutting board. A soft wood is an excellent material for cutting board because the knife will not deflect while leather is being cut. Another material for cutting board is a rubber sheet that is not too soft nor too hard. Please refer to the different kinds of knives listed on the topic TOOLS for a better choice of the knife to use.

C) ***Moistening leather for tooling and carving –***
If you intend to use tooling or carving on your
project, a tooling leather must be used. A vegetable
tanned type of leather can hold the impression of
the design once you moisten the top grain part
of the leather. Observe the following procedures
in moistening the leather; 1) When pieces of the
project have been cut, remove the dust from the
grain side with a dump cloth. 2) Moisten the flesh
side of the lightweight leather with a sponge and
cold water. 3) As soon as you notice that the flesh
side darkens, the moisture content of the leather
has been reached. Moisten the entire piece of
leather so that the shrinkage or color change
will be uniform. When working on heavy leather
which will be used for example on insole or ladies
sandal, soak the entire piece of the cut insole into
a basin of water. Then cover it up or wrap it up in
a cotton towel for several hours or even or even
overnight to make the fiber of the leather swell
and make the heavy leather soft and ready for
tooling or carving.

MAKING SURFACE DESIGNS

D) **_Stamping_** – This is the simplest method of decorating the surface your project. There are many types of stamping tools. Select which one you want to use. Start first with a simple design and then once you acquire the skill, you can proceed and develop a more complicated design. Follow this procedure: 1) Select a design of stamping tool you want to use. You may put the design on a piece of paper or you can have it in your imagination. 2) You can practice first making the design on a scrap leather to make sure that you like the design you have in mind. 3) Moisten the leather and wait until natural color of the leather return. 4) Place the project on a marble slab and holding the stamping tool, strike the tool with a mallet. DO NOT CUT THROUGH the leather with the stamping tool.(See insert of different stamping designs for your reference).

E) ***Outline tooling*** – In outline tooling, only the outline of the design is pressed down. This particular process is good in making monograms or making geometrical designs on bookmarkers, dog collars and many similar projects. Follow the following steps: 1)After making the design, transfer it on the leather by moistening the top grain. 2) Place the leather on a marble slab and go over the outline of the design several times with the smaller end of the modeler. 3) Stop pressing the outline until the lines are depressed at the desired depth. NOTE: Be sure that you keep the depth of the depressed lines uniform. 4) Should the water ooze while tracing the design, allow the leather to dry a little. Leather which is too damp or wet will not hold the impression you are doing. If the modeler tends to scratch or break through the surface of your leather, it means that the moisture of the leather is not enough, so dampen the leather again with a not so wet sponge.

F) ***Flat Modeling*** – This method means that you are depressing or beveling down the background of the design to ensure that the real design stands out in bold relief. Follow this steps: 1) Transfer the design. 2) Start pressing the outline of the design by using the broad end of the modeler. 3) As you see the relief image of the design, begin depressing the background of the design. A deer foot modeler may be used for putting down the background. NOTE: Used a firm and even pressure in depressing the background. 4) You can soften the edges of the design by using the broad end of the modeler to smooth them off. 5) Again, should the leather becomes too dry, moisten it again with a wet sponge.

G) **Stippling the background** - This means that the background of the design is to be decorated by small dot like impressions. By stippling the background you can put more accent on the design. The following steps should be followed: 1) Follow the same steps in making outline tooling. 2) Use different tools such as a tracers, stylus, or the small end of the modeler. 3) Hold your tool in a vertical position and turn it as you apply pressure. BE careful not to break through the outer surface of the leather. NOTE: A stippling tool is recommended in this procedure since stippler covers a greater area that you are depressing.

H) *Carving* - This method of decorating leather is sometimes known as incising, stamping or tooling. Saddle stamps are used to put down the background and to decorate the design. There is no definite procedure in carving but the methods mentioned in earlier in this topic such as stamping, flat modeling, and stippling background can be a good practice for a beginner. Majority of the design used in this process are called western floral design. As you can see in the drawing or design the relief image is a giant size flower. NOTE: It is very, very important for a beginner to practice first on scrap leather the different tools mentioned here in order to achieve the professional look of the design. Remember, any cut, any impression of the stamping tools or modeling tools on the leather **cannot** be erased or correct it. Likewise, study carefully how the different tools in this particular topic are used and see the effects on the design. By looking on the effects of the tools on the design you can have an idea as to how handle the tools to get the desired effects.

I) *Punching Holes* - You make holes to the leather for the following reasons: 1) To provide stitching or lacing lines. This means the holes that will be punched will be say, about ½" or 3/16" from the edge of the project where the lace or the thread will be inserted with the help of a needle in order to put together the different parts of the project being made. 2) You punch holes to place snaps, rivets, grommets and other metal accessories and fittings like the tongue of buckles. For beginners, I strongly suggest that you use a hand held punchers.

Procedure in making holes for fasteners

All holes for belts and for fastener are made either with a rotary puncher or hand held puncher. Follow the following steps;

1) Decide what size of hole will be made. Then mark the leather where the holes will fall.

   In marking the leather, use either a pencil or ball point pen or an awl or ice pick.

2) Position the puncher where hole will be made.

3) Hit the puncher with the mallet or piece of hard wood.

4) For larger holes like attaching sandal straps, depending on the shape of the strap, either a round, oval, or oblong a hand held or drive puncher is used.

5) If a rivet is used for fastener, insert the head of the rivet on the hole which is on the grain side of the leather and insert the other half of the rivet under the head of the rivet and then hit the head to join or fasten the two pieces together.

J) ***Stitching and Lacing*** - This process is used to put together the different parts of your project. Putting the different part of the project is sometimes called assembling.

Assembling Or Joining Pieces Together

Assembling means putting the different pieces of the project together. There are many ways to do this. Either by putting rivet, lacing which is called thonging in some countries and sewing either by hand or machine. For the purpose of this book, will just discuss basic lacing techniques and hand sewing. It is my belief that once the beginner becomes adept and becomes involve in working with leather, using a sewing machine is the penultimate goal.

Lacing – this involve threading or inserting narrow strip of leather through holes or slit in order to hold two or more pieces together. Number of holes to be punched where lace will pass depends on, 1) thickness and/or softness of the leather and how will lace affect the aesthetic look of the project. The rule of thumb is to first layout the holes or slits on the pattern before punching them to the leather. From here visualize how lace will affect the look of your project. Always use a divider to layout and spacing the holes. To lace a project, you need a hole puncher or slit chisel, scissor and needle. You will also need a separate piece of leather to be used as a lace. The width of the lace is equals to the diameter of the hole of the puncher or slit. To make a lace, simply cut a circular piece of leather about 5 inches in diameter and begin cutting on the side having in mind the width that you want to have. Continue cutting in circular motion all the way until leather is done.

Basic lacing stitch technique

Single running stitch

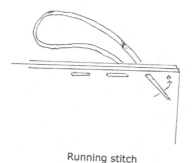

Running stitch

Fig. 7

Single running stitches are made by pulling the lace through each successive holes. Before starting, tie a knot at the end of the lace to prevent the entire lace "running" to the other holes. If you want the knot of the other hole end up on the same spot where the first knot is located, make an even number of holes on the project. Remember, the length of the lace for this particular lace stitch is 1 ½ longer than the seam or length of the project to be laced. Once finished, tie a knot on the end of the lace to prevent the lace from coming out of the seam.

b) Double running or lock stitch

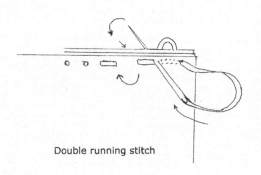

Double running stitch

Fig. 8

Double running lacing stitches are made exactly as single running stitch except that after going through the last hole, continue lace back around in the opposite direction going through again through each hole second time. Upon reaching the hole where you started, tie both ends of lace. The length of the lace for this kind of lacing is twice the length of the distance to be lace.

Whip stitch

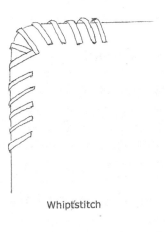

Whip stitch

Fig. 9

Whip lacing stitches are made by putting the lace end through the first hole, over the edge, and through the next holes. Length of the lace is three times the distance to be laced.

Double running whip stitch

Double whipstitches

Fig. 10

Double whip lace stitch is the same as above except that instead of going directly to the next hole, you pass the lace on the same hole twice. The length of the lace is twice the distance of the length that will be laced. Note: There are several ways to keep the lace from going undone. 1) tie the ends of the knots, 2) while you pull the lace all the way through first hole, leave a short length of the other end of lace remain on one side. Then bend this end against the direction you are lacing and make the second and third stitches over it. Finish seam by pulling the end of the lace back under the last several stitches. NOTE : In lacing around corner, go twice through the two of the holes or slits.

Single Loop or Single Overlay

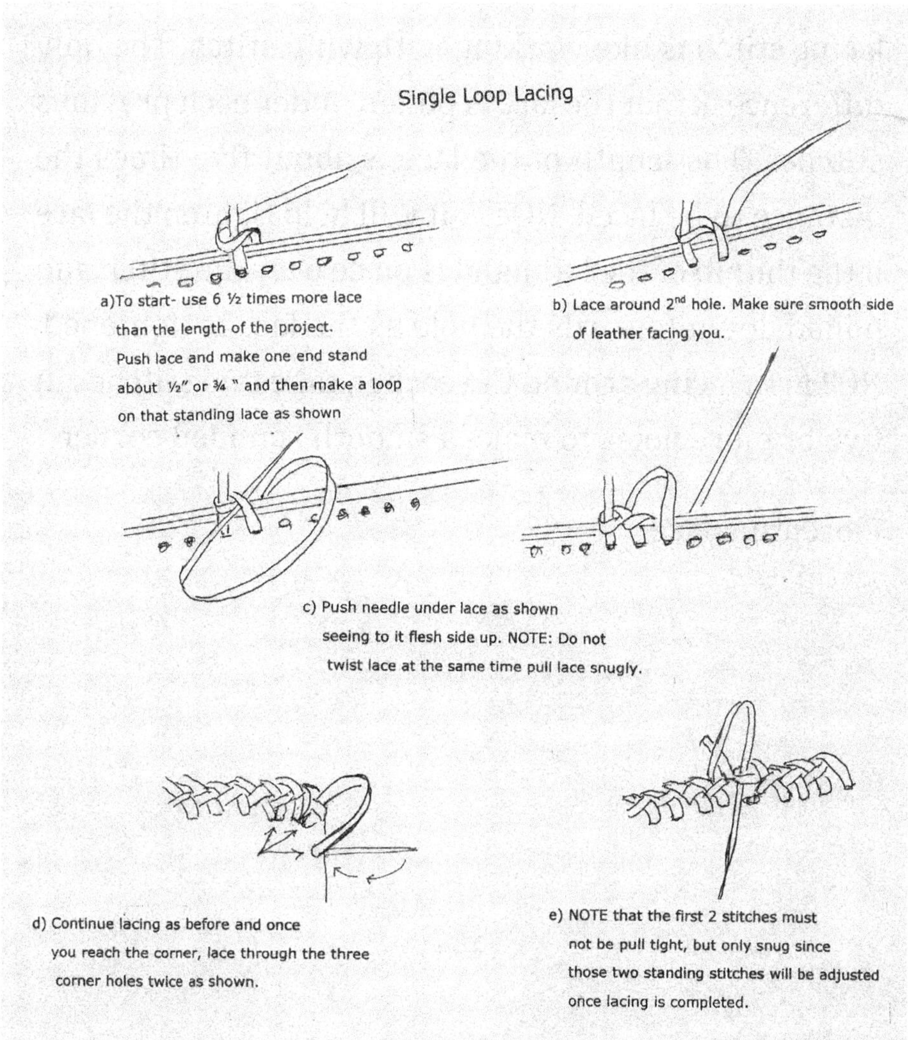

Single Loop Lacing

a) To start- use 6 ½ times more lace
than the length of the project.
Push lace and make one end stand
about ½" or ¾ " and then make a loop
on that standing lace as shown

b) Lace around 2nd hole. Make sure smooth side
of leather facing you.

c) Push needle under lace as shown
seeing to it flesh side up. NOTE: Do not
twist lace at the same time pull lace snugly.

d) Continue lacing as before and once
you reach the corner, lace through the three
corner holes twice as shown.

e) NOTE that the first 2 stitches must
not be pull tight, but only snug since
those two standing stitches will be adjusted
once lacing is completed.

Fig. 11 - Making a Single Loop Lacing

This kind of lacing cover the edges of the leather with a decorative pattern. Working on this kind of lacing stitch is like working with whip stitch. The only difference is that the lace is pulled under each previous stitches. The length of the lace is about five times the distance to be laced. NOTE: It will help tighten the lace if the thumb of the left hand is place over the stitch and pulled down towards the hole as the lace is tightened. NOTE: In lacing around the corner, take two stitches in two or more holes to make a smooth rounded corner.

Florentine lace

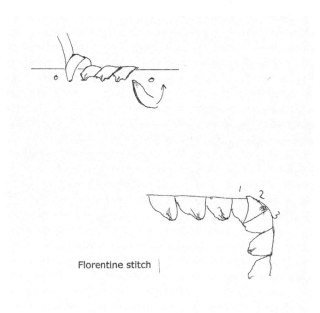

Florentine stitch

Fig. 12

The effect of this lace stitching is much different from the rest.

Use a smaller hole for a wider width lace. The lace should be thin like a kid skin. Tapered the end of the lace and have a pointed end. No needle necessary for lacing.

Hand Stitching

Hand and machine stitching can be done also on leather just like on fabrics. However, most often, hand stitching is much more superior to machine sewing because stitches can be pulled tighter and therefore will not loose easily compare to machine made lock stitch.

Below is the number of stitches need while working with leather.

Thickness of leather Stitches per inch

1mm or less	12
1.5 mm	10
2.0 to 2.5 mm	8
2.5 to 4.	7
4.0 to 6 mm	7

There are several types of hand stitching and most of them are used in making molded and box type leather articles. And since this book is only for beginners, I will just mention few types or methods.

Automatic awl stitching

Using an automatic stitching awl makes a strong lock stitch. This tool carries a spool of thread which feeds out as you sew. Layout first the holes on the project using the divider. Refer to the number of stitches needed according to the thickness of leather. Once the layout of stitches were done, follow the following procedure;

Unscrew the top of the handle which has the wrench and the needle. Note: When you buy this tool the reel of thread is already set up and with instructions.

1) Put the needle in the shank with groove on the same side of the thread that comes out of the reel of thread.

2) Tighten the shank with the awl wrench while holding the needle.

2a) When threading the needle, be sure that the thread follows groove of needle.

3) Return the wrench on top of the handle and tighten it.

4) Pierce the leather and pull the thread all the way through the other side of the project. This act as bobbin thread for the stitching. The length of the thread is twice the distance to be sewn.

5) Push the needle through the leather where the next stitch is to be made and draw it half way out, to create a loop in the thread along the needle.

6) Pass the end of the thread now acting as the bobbin through the loop and with draw the needle completely. Note: Hold the reel so that it will not turn.

7) Both ends of the thread are then pulled equally tight so that the loop between the two pieces of the leather will lay flat.

Using stitching Awl

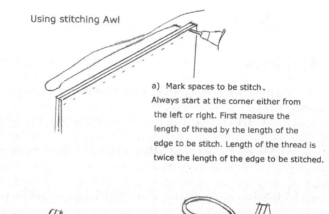

a) Mark spaces to be stitch.
Always start at the corner either from
the left or right. First measure the
length of thread by the length of the
edge to be stitch. Length of the thread is
twice the length of the edge to be stitched.

b) After pulling up the thread from the first hole
go the second hole leaving the other end of the thread
at the back of the project.

c) After the needle had passed the second hole,
insert the other end of the thread to the loop.

d) Once both thread lay flat at the project,
pull both ends of thread.

Fig. 13 – Using Stitching Awl

Back stitch – Using one needle, this similar to running stitch lacing except that instead of sewing each stitch directly in front of the previous one, you bring the needle back to the last hole and go through again before sewing forward. See illustration carefully.

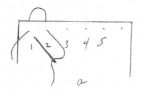

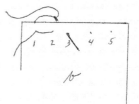

Start backstitches like running stitches but drop
back the needle to previous stitch before continuing
forward.

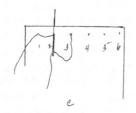

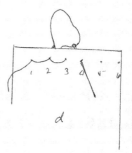

Fig. 14 – Back Stitching

Double running or lock stitch - using two needles
with thread running the needle simultaneously in two
holes like what you do with lacing.

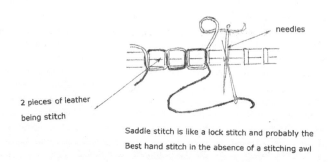

needles

2 pieces of leather
being stitch

Saddle stitch is like a lock stitch and probably the
Best hand stitch in the absence of a stitching awl

Fig. 15 – saddle Stitch or Double Needle Stitching

DESCRIPTION AND PROCEDURE ON HOW TO USE THE DIFFERENT STAMPING TOOLS

Procedure on how to use the camouflage stamping tool - 1) If you are right handed, use your left hand thumb and index finger with the middle finger and ring finger holding the tool. Your ring finger rest on the leather. See to it that the tool should not quite touch the material (leather). 2) With your elbow resting on the table, tap the tool with a mallet or striking wood. See to it again that once you strike or tap the tool it will "spring" back in holding position. Your finger will act as the spring.

Procedure in using the Pear Shader stamping tool - This tool comes in different sizes and is used to depress certain areas of the design to give more depth, add contour and create a more realistic appearance. It might be smooth, checkered or ribbed. With this design, it will be a personal choice of what to use. Bear in mind that this tool is use to produce shaded effect on leaves and petals. Follow the following procedure : - *1)* Hold this stamping tool the same way you hold other stamping tool. 2) Hit this tool slightly tilted in order to produce tapered depression. See to it that the depression is uniformly away from the cut made by the swivel knife.

Procedure in using the beveler - Which side should be beveled? All the areas where designs should stand out or should be seen bold. Small bevelers are used in close areas and the large ones are used along straight cuts and large curves. Follow the following instructions: 1) Hold the tool similar to the other tools while you put the thick part of this tool along the cut done swivel knife. 2) Move this tool along the cut seeing to it that you made a smooth and deep bevel. 3) You can taper the bevel as you come close the end of the design or cut. NOTE: A rule of thumb; always bevel outside the cut and away from the design you want to stand out.

Procedure in using the veiner - This stamping tool is like the vein of a leaf of a stem. Hence, the word veiner. It is suggested that in order to create a good impression, practice how to apply different pressure in order to get the right impression you want to create. Further, it would be better to tilt the tools while stamping. Using this tools is like using the other stamping tools.

Procedure in using the seeder - This stamping tool is used to create the impression of a pollen or seed of the flower, the reason why this is used at the center of a flower design. To use this tool, hold the stamping tool upright and strike the tool firmly to have a good impression. You can also tilts one side of this tool if you think you can create a better design.

It is not feasible to discuss how to use all the stamping tools to make a good carving, Perhaps, it would be better to for the first timer to practice first and then move on in making more complex design as you gain the experience. The purpose of introducing these carving tools to you is for you to know them and how they are use. Then practice, practice, practice.

Finishing Up The Project

MAKING BORDER LINE

If the edge of your project will be not be finished with out lacing, like men's belt, then the edges can have border line. Border line is parallel to the edge of the project. This border line can be done by the use of the modeling tool guided by a ruler. However, if edger is available this tool will be very useful if there are curve edges. In using the edger on a tooling leather, see to it that you have moisten the leather first. Then place the right foot of the edger outside the edge of the leather and then use the left foot of the edger in marking the leather moving the tool using your left forefinger as a guide.

GUSSETS

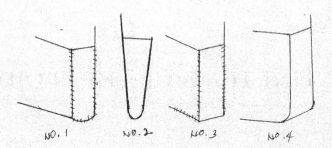

NO. 1   NO. 2   NO. 3   NO. 4

Fig. 16 – Kinds of Gussets

No.1) Front and back of the bag are cut in one piece. The edge of the gusset which is rounded is placed around the edge. Note how lace is done. 2) If you preferred, gusset can be cut wider on top to make it easier to get things inside the bag. 3) and 4 – A continuous gusset consisting of a strip of leather extending to one end of the project and the bottom and up of the other side. Note: Lower corner of the sides of the project can be a square or can be rounded.

This is a piece of leather placed along the side of the project to make the space inside the project wider so that whatever thing is inside, those can be reached and remove easily.

Gussets can be stitched in by machine on very thin leather or can also be hand stitch or laced. In order to understand the function of the gusset the author have include a small project using this kind of assembly.

LINING

There are certain leather goods that appears to have better quality if there is lining., Lining are those found inside ladies handbags or in formal leather shoes. It is made up of silk or imitations suede or genuine suede made from sheep skin. The cheapest leather lining is the pigskin or the imitation calfskin. To better understand the use of lining, the author have added a project using lining. NOTE; Lining is usually cut slightly larger than the article to be lined. It is placed upon the cemented surface and rubbed in all directions with your hand or any straight edge piece of wood to remove wrinkles.

DYEING AND FINISHING

Dyeing is only one of the many ways to make any leather article look beautiful. Materials like acrylic, oil, lacquer based finished and even shoe polish are used to make your project attractive. There are certain procedures to be done in using any of these *dressing or leather finish materials.* The following procedure should be followed :

1. Before applying any leather dressing or finishing material, see to it that the surface of the leather is clean or free from dust or any foreign material.

2. Tooling design must be completely done or finished before applying color (dye or acrylic)

3. In putting the dye on your project, the entire surface of the leather to be dyed must be cleaned by a mild solution of oxalic acid or ammonia water.

4. To promote even absorption or ensure that the color will be evenly spread, moistened the article. To avoid mistake, experiment this process in a scrap of leather.

5. To obtain an even coloring, apply several light coats of diluted dye and gradually build up the desired color.

6. After putting the dye, you need to "dress" or "finish" the leather.

7. Shoe polish is a dressing material.

8. By pushing a piece of hard wood on a damp leather a "glazed" surface can be obtained. This presses is called "burnishing".

9. As a beginner you must be careful when using dye. It is almost impossible to remove the dye once applied.

10. Small camel's hair brush give satisfactory results in applying dye.

11. If you are using water based dye, brush should be cleaned by washing with soap and water after it has been used.

SNAPS - These are metals commonly used to hold down the flaps of coin purses, handbags, inside pockets of handbags, key cases and any other projects that require "security" for the things found inside the handbags and coin purses. See drawing for the procedure in attaching snaps.

PROCEDURE IN PUTTING SNAPS

1) Looking at the drawing, the snap has 4 parts: For the top parts lets call it A and B.

2) At the Bottom part we call it C and D.

3) Mark where the snap will be placed on **both pieces of the project.**

4) Punch hole on the leather where the size of the hole should be same as the B

5) Place B under the wrong side of the leather(the flesh side) and place A which is like a cap on the right side or grain side of the leather **on top of B.**

6) Place the concave cylinder of your snap setter on A and hit it with a mallet.

7) Now, for the other half. With hole on the second piece of the project just matching the place where A and B is located, place D on the flesh side of the leather.

8) Place C on top of D (C should be on the right side or the grain of leather) and with the smaller cylinder of the snap setter tap C with a mallet.

NOTE; Every time you tap the snap or hit the snap with a mallet, do it in a some what" milder" hit in order not to crash the snap or prevent the C part be inserted on B part.

Hitting should be firm just enough make all part of snap **NOT** rotating or moving.

METAL FITTINGS

Aside from snaps, there are a variety of metal fittings used to close flaps, attached straps or handles or join pieces together. The photo of metal fittings will give you an idea as where these metal fittings are used. There are locks, that serve just like snaps, rivets, buckles, rings and studs. As you progress in your skill in making leather items, these metals will be used since these are the things that made leather goods beautiful.

PROCEDURE IN PUTTING A RIVET

Rivets are commonly used to fastened/join pieces or parts of you project. Rivets comes in two parts, "male" and "female". The "female" part has a cap and the "male" is the other half. To insert rivets:

1) Punch a hole on the two pieces of leather you wish to join. Size of the hole should match the "female" part of the rivet.

NOTE; Be sure to know before hand where the "male" part or the "female" part will be placed. Should it be on the wrong side of the leather? Example is when you are working on a belt where the buckle will be placed. Sometimes when you will be working on a sandal or a handbag be sure to know where the "male" and "female" will be placed.'

2) Insert the "male" part on the hole either on the wrong side or the grain side.

3) Place the "female" part over the "male" part and then hit the female part with a mallet or hammer. NOTE: Hit the rivet with a "milder" stroke to prevent the rivet from being crushed.

GROMMETS

Grommets are sturdy and is like a two piece eyelet. They are used for lacing and decorations, and can be used through two thicknesses of leather.

PROCEDURE IN INSERTING GROMMETS

1. Mark the leather where the grommet will be placed.

2. Get a drive punch that matches the size of the grommet. NOTE: The best way to match the drive punch is to slide the grommet into the drive punch to make sure it fits properly.

3. Punch hole on the leather where grommet will be placed.

4. Place the larger half of the grommet into the base of the grommet setter. NOTE: Place the leather so that the hole is right over the grommet right side down.

5. Place the remaining part of the grommet into the hole and cover with the top of the grommet setter.

6. Top the setter firmly with a mallet.

EYELETS

Eyelets are sometimes used as a decoration or as a protection for holes specially in ladies belts.

1. Mark your project where you will put the eyelet.

2. Punch the leather matching the diameter of the "foot" of the eyelet.

3. Put the eyelet on the right side or grain of the leather

4. Invert the project

Planning And Preparing Items Or Projects To Be Made

In planning and preparing items or projects to be made, it is needed to consider that there are some leather items or goods that had been used for a long time. Examples of these are; cigarette cases, wallets, purses or handbags or sometimes known also as book bags. What is then needed is to think of a different design that will blend or go with what is in fashion or mood. Women belts and handbags or book bags are very sensitive to fashion and therefore the design must be "at tune" with what is "in" in terms of what is prevailing at the time of manufacture or the time when the item will be sold. Aside from design, color, sizes and other features such as the decorative metals or locks has to be consider also. Likewise, from time to time, men's belt also goes in fashion in terms of width. Question like what is the prevailing design or width has to be considered. Is the width narrow or wide? Perhaps there would be a design on the edges or would be plain color.

Then what color? Will it be black, brown, or burgundy? The other most important thing to consider is the type of material to be used. What kind of leather is now in fashion? Remember, the things mentioned above will greatly influence the buyers.

In order to guide the prospective leather goods maker on the different items that are saleable or in case the designer or maker who want to go export, the following table is valuable as this table was prepared by no less than the UNITED NATIONS CENTER FOR TRADE AND DEVELOPMENT (UNCTAD).

CUSTOMER OF LEATHER GOODS PREFERENCES ACCORDING TO GROUP AND AGES

GROUP ACCORDING TO AGES PREFERENCES IN BUYING

From 15 to 30 years old Items bought by this group is what we called in "fashion", especially those 19 yrs. olds. Craftsmanship must be high quality as price is not an issue for them.

From 31 to 50 years old   Style is not daring, but with a "classic" taste. Which means design must either be innovative, if not original.

From 51 to 64 years old Customers in this group looks at the functionality of leather good they are buying. People in this group are looking for durability and of quality. Design is not so important. This group wants a modest rate price.

TO ENCOURAGE FUTURE EXPORTERS, BELOW IS THE PEAK SEASON FOR BUYERS OF LEATHR GOODS

ITEM	PERIOD OF PEAK SALE
Gloves, Women's Handbags	January and February
Fashion bag, Small leather goods	March and April
Travel goods, luggage	June and July
Women's handbags, schoolbags	In Europe and USA: August and September
	In the Philippines: May and June
Women's handbags, luggage	October
Small leather goods, travel goods	November
Travel goods, gift items, gloves	December

PART II

Suggested Projects

The items presented here are small items. It intends to gain a first hand knowledge of using tools and to have experience of using the right materials. From these small items the beginners can move forward to more stylist and fashionable items as it is assume that the beginner has "grown" or gain "knack" of the leather goods manufacture.

Book Mark

There are 2 different sizes presented here. The student can pick which one is the best type to begin with. Remember, this is the time to practice your artistic taste as well as develop your skills.

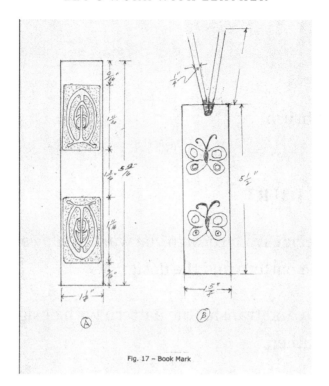

Fig. 17 – Book Mark

Material Needed:

2 or 3 oz. tooling Leather

Dye of different colors

Tools Needed;

Cutting knife

Stamping tools or modeler

Steel rule

Mallet

Stylus

Paint brush

PROCEDURE

1) Decide which design you want to copy and make the pattern and the design.

2) Cut and transfer the pattern with design on the leather.

3) Moisten the leather.

4) Trace the design on the leather.

5) Use your stamping tools or modeling in making design.

6) You can finish the project by staining or coloring the design.

7) Do not forget to color the edges.

Luggage Tag

There are 2 different designs to choose from. Just to let the beginner know that the purpose of this project is to understand how to join pieces together and practice in making surface design.

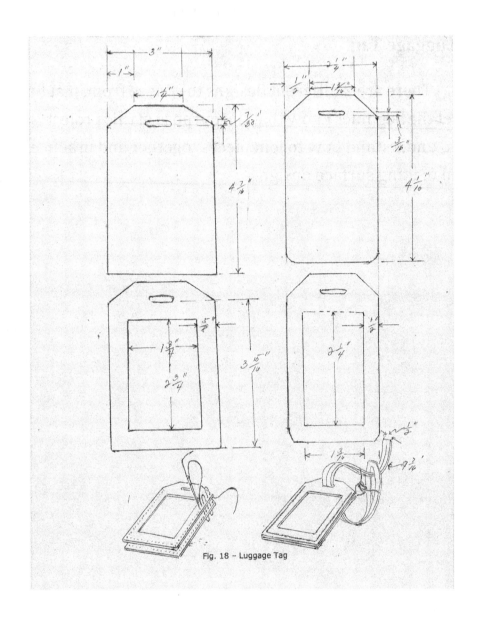

Fig. 18 – Luggage Tag

Materials Needed:

1) Tooling Leather from 3 to 5 oz

2) Buckle or snap

3) Dye

4) Contact cement

Tools Needed:

Cutting Knife

Stamping tools or modeler

Mallet

Steel Rule

Snap Setter

PROCEDURE

1) Choose the design and dimension you want then make the pattern.

2) Transfer the pattern on the leather (smooth side on top and the flesh side at the bottom)

3) Cut the leather according to the pattern. The portion where "window" is located should be cut first. Then cut the second portion. NOTE: On picture no. 2 small tag has a dotted line on

top. This means you may or may not cut that portion. If you decide not to cut that portion the "window" has a "cover" in order to protect the identity of the owner from a third party

4) Once the second portion (part) has been cut then moisten the surface of that portion. Make the surface design. Is it tooling or curving?

5) Once design has been made, cut the strap and cut the hole intended for the strap as indicated in the pattern.

6) Start assembling the project by applying contact cement at the edges of the project.

7) Using the divider, start laying out the holes needed for stitching or lacing.

8) Punch holes using the appropriate diameter. For hand stitching hole should be1/6 to 1/8 inch but for hand lacing should be 1/4 inch. Note: The diameter of the hole for lacing should be the width of the lace.

9) For hand stitching you need a big needles and thread. Length of the thread is twice the perimeter of the project.

10) Procedure in Hand Stitching:

a) Put the one end of the thread on the needle. Start between layers leaving at least 1 ½" to 2" of thread to tie off later. Stitch thru the first hole of front part leaving the other end of thread between layers as shown on drawing A.

b) Push the needle up through first hole and stitch on second hole

c) Push the needle down from the second hole. Then stitch thru the third hole.

d) Pull stitch tight.

e) When you reach the last hole. Turn and stitch back around till you reach the starting point. You will notice that all holes are filled up.

f) Upon reaching the starting point, stitch through the hole at the back part and bring the thread out between front and back (see drawing B).

g) Tie thread ends in a knot and at the same time pulling them down between layers. Trim or cut excess thread.

h) Insert plastic on the open part of the front part

i) Make strap with buckle or make strap as shown on drawing B.

Wristband

This project is presented to introduce the beginner the type of decoration he/she can make on the surface of the leather. Aside from the traditional tooling and stamping, the beginner can use a decorative puncher (see picture) or decorative "hardwares" or Supplies such as rivets, rings, diamond shape studs etc.

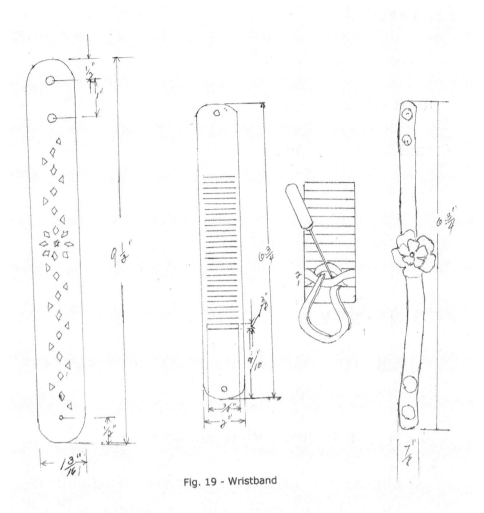

Fig. 19 - Wristband

Materials Needed:

1) 3 oz. veg. tanned leather

2) Snap

3) Dye color of your choice

Tools Needed:

Cutting knife or scissor

Rivet setter

Modeler or stamping tools

Mallet

Decorative Puncher (if needed)

PROCEDURE

1) Cut the leather according to specs or measurement.

2) Wet the leather with clean water.

3) Choose the method of surface design. Is it tooling?, stamping? or decorative punches? or putting studs?

4) Work on the method of surface design.

5) Let leather dry and finish your work by putting dye and put snaps at the end of the strap.

COIN PURSE WITH GUSSET

NOTE: The purpose of this project is to make the beginner aware of how he/she can make a wider room for the leather item either with a coin purse or a ladies handbag. Gusset is always put on the side of the leather item. Most of the time, to secure the inside part of the leather item specially ladies handbags, a zipper or snap is placed. I put only one size of this project but the beginner is always free to have his/her discretion on the size and the design to be put on the project. Likewise, the beginner should know that zipper can be either be sewed manually or with a stitching machine. On this project, you can place the zipper on the gusset manually using your needle and a regular thread. The stitch is about 6 to 7 stiches per inch.

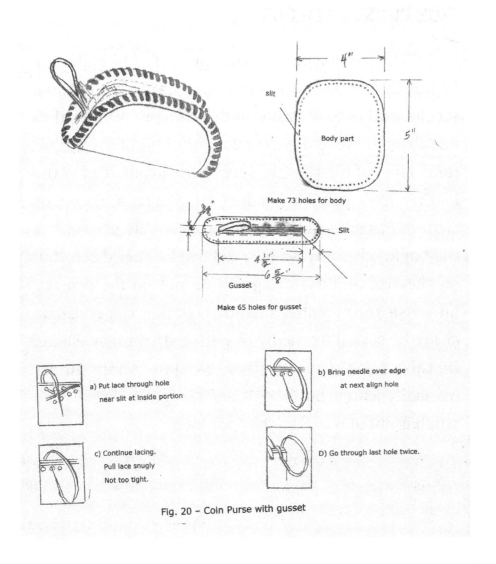

slit

Body part

4"

5"

Make 73 holes for body

Slit

Gusset

4 1/8"

6 5/8"

Make 65 holes for gusset

a) Put lace through hole near slit at inside portion

b) Bring needle over edge at next align hole

c) Continue lacing. Pull lace snugly Not too tight.

D) Go through last hole twice.

Fig. 20 – Coin Purse with gusset

Materials Needed:

1) 5" brown zipper

2) 3 oz. vegetable tanned leather

3) Regular big needle and thread

4) 1/8" lace

5) Dye (Brown)

Tools Needed:

1) Scissor

2) Cutting knife

3) Puncher 1/8 inch diameter

4) Mallet

5) Stamping tools

6) Sewing machine

PROCEDURE

1. Make pattern as shown.

2. Layout pattern on smooth side of the leather

3. Layout holes. Body part or the outside part have 73 holes including slit and gusset has 65 holes including slit.

4. Cut center part of gusset where zipper will be place. Noticed the "handle" at the left side of the cut piece. This handle was made by joining the right hand cut piece to the left side uncut piece.

5. Attach zipper.

6. Align the slit of the gusset with the slit of the outside part.

7. Start lacing as describe on drawings A to D.

LINK BELT

NOTE: There are myriad of small leather items or projects that you can make. I just hope that the most important thing that you gained is the inspiration of making things out of leather. Also, the beginner got the idea on how to decorate the surface of the leather.

Another type of leather item that a beginner can make is belt. This time, I am presenting a different kind of belt. This project can be made from scrap from shoe upper of ladies shoes. This scraps or sometimes known as remnants are chrome tanned and with colors already. Scraps or remnants can be obtained free of charge from factories that make ladies shoes. You can also use the full size upper vegetable tanned leather. The only thing in using this type of leather requires you to apply dye. Most common color for men's belt are brown or black. If you intend to make link belt for women, using the vegetable tanned leather you can apply dye different kind of color other than brown or black.

NOTE: At the opposite page, notice that actual size of Link is included. However, due to space limitation make your own pattern for tongue or otherwise know as Belt Billet End. There is also the Buckle End where the buckle can be placed. The measurements used in both parts are based on the actual size of the Link.

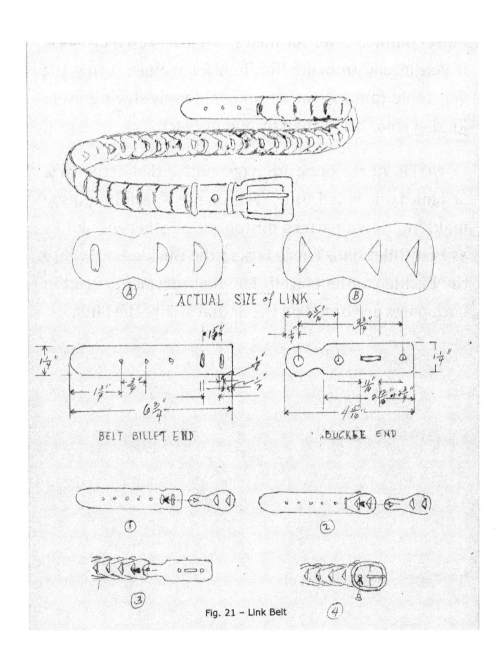

ACTUAL SIZE of LINK

Ⓐ   Ⓑ

BELT BILLET END

BUCKLE END

① ② ③ ④

Fig. 21 – Link Belt

78

Materials Needed:

Buckle – 1 ¼ inch wide (inside measurement)

Rivet

Snap Button

3 oz. Chrome tanned upper leather use remnants from ladies shoes

3 or 4 oz. vegetable tanned leather natural color dye

Tools Needed:

A) Scissor

B) Oblong hole puncher or in the absence of this kind of puncher, improvise by making a chisel like cutter using a 5 or 6 inch common nail and shape the tip of this nail like a chisel or screw driver. Make this sharp in order to cut the thickness of the leather.

C) 1/8 inch hole puncher for the rivet

D) Mallet

PROCEDURE

1) Copy the specifications or drawing of the different parts as shown.

2) Cut the pieces on the cardboard as this will serve as your pattern. Note: Take a closer look at the Link. Link A has a straight edge while Link B has somewhat circular or curve edge. Select whichever edge you want to use. Just remember that if you choose the straight edge link, the edges of the belt once finished will look like straight. Whereas, the curve edge will produce a wavy edge. That's the difference of the two Link pattern.

3) Transfer the pattern on the leather.

4) Cut the pieces accordingly.

   Take note of the cut portion inside the Link. The cut inside the Link can either be a triangle or semi-circle. Decide which one to use.

5) For the Belt Billet End or Tongue and the Buckle End, use the 4 oz. leather. Transfer the pattern for the Belt Billet End and the Buckle End on this leather.

Now, either take your favorite belt or measure your own waist or have somebody measure your waist to get the exact measurement of your waist.

To get your waist length for the belt; your measurement number from the tape measure add about 5 or 6 inches equals the length of your belt.

If you will use your favorite belt, belt length is from the top end of your buckle to the worn hole of the belt plus 4 ½ inches. Use this belt as your guide while making or linking the belt.

Before linking each piece, color or dye the Links according to your taste. However, if you are using the chrome tanned leather, proceed in cutting the holes required on all parts. Once you finish the cutting of holes proceed in linking parts (see drawing 1). Meantime, see to it that smooth side of the leather is facing you. Note also that once the smaller end of Link has been inserted on the second hole bend the Link to align 3 sloths or holes.

6) Fold Link 2 and insert it through the aligned holes (see drawing 2). Pull them again and bend in order to align first and second holes now sandwiched over the last hole of Link 1.

7) Continue inserting Links until you reach the measurement you desire.

8) Attach the Buckle End by bending the round end of the Buckle End in half and insert through the last 3 aligned Link holes (see drawing 3). Pull Link and bend to align with 2nd rivet hole. You can now cut the last hole of the last Link so that all holes are aligned.

9) Attach the buckle by sliding Buckle End up through the buckle. Insert the tongue of the buckle into the hole and fold end aligning all 3 rivet holes.

10) Attach the rivet or Chicago Screw if you have it (see drawing 4).

Ladies Belt

NOTE : Making ladies belts is a challenge. Since this item is fashionable, the kind and texture of the material, color, design and accessories plays an important factor for this kind of product. It is in this reason that I included this project. I want to point out about color combination and the usefulness of this item. Likewise other kind of material can be used in this project.

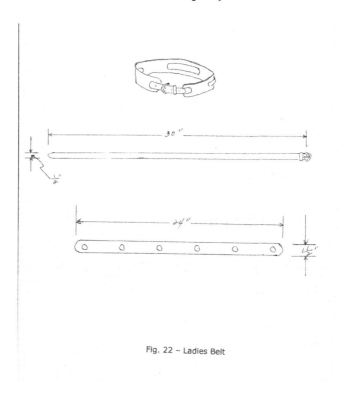

Fig. 22 – Ladies Belt

Materials Needed:

3 0z. vegetable tanned tooling leather (this should be dyed and with or without surface design depending on your concept). Remember, this project should have two color combination I suggest use complimentary

colors like white and black, brown and beige or red and blue or vice versa.

Belt Buckle with ½ inch width either in gold, nickel plated or antique finished.

Grommet – Should match with the color of the buckle.

Rivet - finished of rivet should match the color of the buckle.

Tools Needed:

Scissor or cutting knife

Hole Puncher ½ inch and 1/8 inch for the tongue of the buckle

Rivet Setter

Steel Rule

P R O C E D U R E:

1) Measure the waist line of the would be wearer or use her favorite belt or you can get her favorite belt so that you can get the exact measurement

of the waist or the hole where the tongue of the buckle will be placed.

2) Using the drawing you can make the pattern.

3) Transfer the pattern on the true surface of the leather and cut.

4) Working on the narrow piece, put the buckle on one end and attached it only with one rivet.

5) Using the same color of the narrow piece make a belt keeper. Belt keeper is the small narrow band that holds the belt in place. See drawing.

6) Once belt keeper is made, insert that into the belt near the first rivet that is holding the buckle and attach the second rivet. That will make the belt keeper at the middle of the two rivets.

7) Work on the wider belt by marking where the first piece will be threaded or inserted.

8) Finish the work by punching hole on the narrow piece where the tongue of the buckle will be inserted which is the true waist line of wearer.

9) You can put dye on the edge of the two belts.

LADIES SHOULDER HANDBAG (WITH GUSSET)

The most fashionable leather goods item. There are millions of designs, materials that can be used as well as "hardwares" or decorative materials that can be used in this project. If you are thinking of business this is the most profitable of all items.

However, I will cover only the most basic in order to understand the principle in making ladies handbags. I believe the design here is "universal" and even the method of assembly is the simplest so as to make the beginner discover the underlying principle in making handbags.

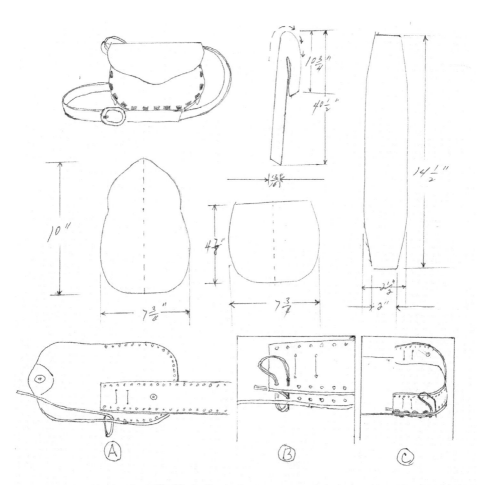

Fig. 23 – Ladies shoulder bag (with gusset)

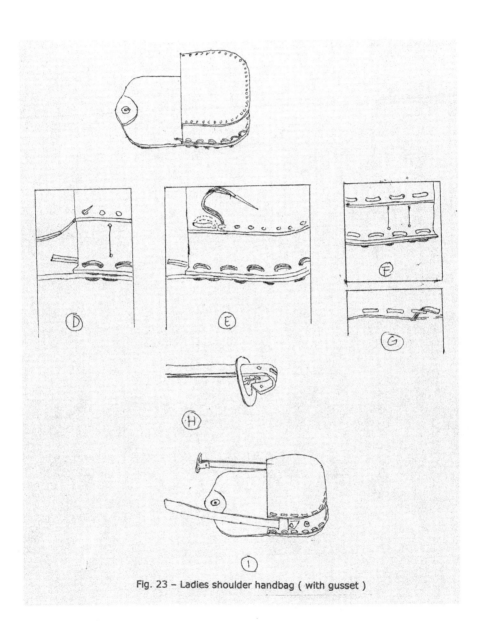

Fig. 23 – Ladies shoulder handbag (with gusset)

Materials Needed :

4 oz. soft vegetable tanned leather

Lacing needle

Magnetic snap (sometimes called claps)

Rivet

Fashionable buckle

Big snap that will hold the shoulder strap

Manual hole puncher

Mallet

Nail Chisel (fashioned like a ¼" screw driver) use a 5 or 6 inches common

nail

Cutting knife or scissor

PROCEDURE

1) Make the necessary patterns as shown. Then label each part.

2) Make/cut the lace according the diameter of the hole puncher.

3) Transfer pattern on the leather (true side or smooth side only). Include the tabs (a piece of leather that will be used to cover the prongs or "feet" of the claps) for both the magnetic snaps or claps (for female and male snaps).

4) To lay out holes, temporarily glue the front and back part, then using a divider layout holes.

5) Note: You only laid out hole for the front and back of the bag but not with the holes for the gusset. To do this, transfer the laid out holes of the front part to the gusset by laying the same holes thru a divider or "wrapping" around the gusset to the front part and try to transfer each holes one by one.

6) Do the same thing to the back part.

7) Once holes were laid out for **both** back and front parts, transferred those laid holes to the gusset (see to it that these holes tally with or in sync with the holes of both front and back parts of the bag), punch holes on all parts including that of

the strap handle. Do not forget to make the holes for the rivet and buckle on the strap.

8) Dye or put coloring on all parts including edges and the flesh side of leather.

Note: Put a light color on the flesh side.

9) Make slits on both ends of the gusset for the handle straps. (See drawing I)

10) Place the female magnetic snap (claps) on the front part of the bag. You can do this by making slits using a 6" common nail fashioned as screw driver or chisel, where you can insert the prongs of the magnetic snap (claps). **Note:** to be able to determine the exact place where to put the claps, fold the pattern of the front part of the bag lengthwise and get the center. After getting the center, mark it and from the top of the front part, measure at least 1" from the top and put mark. The center of the claps should "sit" at the center of the pattern, while the 2 prongs or feet of the claps are located at both sides of the center. Transfer this "location" to the back part of the pattern and eventually to the leather. Now you can place the female magnetic claps or snap

11) Place the male magnetic snap (claps) at the flap of back part and place it on the **flesh side** (see drawing A).

12) Cover the prongs or feet of the claps both male and female with tab or piece of leather to avoid leather being scratch by the prongs.

13) Start lace stitching at the back part. (See drawing A) To start, stitch or lace down on hole 2 at the back part only, then stitch the lace up in hole 1 on both the back part and the gusset (see drawing B).

14) As soon as lace has been stitch on both sides (gusset and back part) by stitching down the lace from hole one to hole 2 on the gusset side (see drawing B) tightly pull the lace and align all holes.

15) Continue stitching the lace up to the last hole of both gusset and back part (see drawing C).

16) Once you reach the last hole, stitch tight the lace and cut (the lace).

17) Put the front part of he bag.

18) Coming from the inside of the front part, stitch lace on hole one of both parts (see drawing D). Again, align the holes.

19) Stitch lace on next hole (see drawing E**). Note:** see how the end of the lace has been tack before proceeding to the next hole.

20) Stitch lace up to the last hole of back and front parts of the bag (see drawing F).

21) At the last hole (inside part of the bag, tack the end of he lace as shown on drawing G.

22) Attach buckle and set rivet on the strap (see drawing).

23) Attach handle straps.

PART III

How to make a Sandal

INTRODUCTION

As mentioned earlier, it is the intention of this book to motivate the reader to move to another level of skill which is sandal making. It is hope that the reader can have a better insight of what we can make from leather.

Sandals are airy and very fashionable. It is a footwear item that defies season and age. Also sandals are inexpensive to make.

As a starter, let me introduce to you the different terms used in footwear making.

1) Instep - this part is found from the ankle the part which receding towards the toes of the foot.

2) Upper - Part of the footwear whether shoes or sandals that hold or binds the instep. For sandals this part is called straps

3) Insole - Part of the footwear where the sole of the foot rest and where the upper is placed

4) Outer sole - The part of the footwear that touches the ground. This is where we attached the Insole.

TOOLS NEEDED

1) Utility knife or shoe knife

2) Cutting knife

3) hole puncher

4) Shoemaker hammer - although any kind of hammer is useful depending on the location of the reader of this book.

5) Electric motor - To be used as a sander to clean the edges of the finished sandal

6) Pencil

7) Steel square (optional)

MATERIALS AND ACCESSORIES NEEDED

1) Upper Leather - Top grain leather more or less ¼ inch thick. Use a natural color upper leather.

2) Canvass - This can be a good substitute for upper leather.

3) Insole Board - for places where shoe material suppliers are accessible this is the right term and the right material to used. Sometimes this is called leather board. NOTE: In places where there is no store for shoe materials, you can use a compressed cardboard that will not disintegrate easily when moisture sets in.

4) Outer Sole - Again for places where there are shoe suppliers, this is the right term and material to used. The reader can select either a rubber sole or a leather sole. Soling materials either rubber or leather is sold by thickness which is called iron. The sales clerk will show you what thickness you need. Usually, thickness starts at 1/2 inch up to 1/4 inch thick. I recommend rubber sole than the leather sole for sandals not only for economic reason but because rubber sole has more traction than leather sole. Now in places

where it is difficult to obtain soling material, a worn out automobile or truck tire is the best. Just remove the hard part of the tire (found near the rim) with a sharp knife and later on cut the tire across the width and strengthen it.

5) Stitching Awl or Big needle - this will be used to join the straps if you will make a Japanese sandal.

Accessories needed

1) Strap buckle - width is same as the width of the strap

2) Rivet - depends on the thickness of the leather

3) Sandpaper - no. 1 or 2

4) Rubber or contact cement

PROCEDURE

Before anything else, decide which style of sandal will you make. Is it a Japanese sandal, a toe sandal or chappal (Indian word for the Toe sandal) or the two-strap sandal with or without the heel strap? Which ever you choose, the procedure will be basically the same. Meantime, upper of sandals are called straps or in some countries is called thongs. It is therefore important to remember that upper straps can be placed in several places. It could be in front or at the back of the large joint of our big toe; and in front or at the back of the joint on the smallest toe and also; at the highest point of our arch, at the instep and across of this point. This is called two straps sandal. NOTE: Arch is located at the bottom of the foot and the instep is the receding portion of our foot from the ankle to the fingers (toe) of the feet. Straps can also be placed between the big toe and the second strap holds the instep. This is called the toe sandal or chappal. The Japanese sandal is where the two pieces of straps are placed at opposite sides of the foot and the other two ends of straps are joined together between the big toe and the next toe.

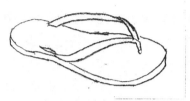

Japanese or Thong Sandal

Chappal or Toe Sandal

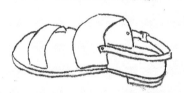

Two strap Sandal with Heel strap

Fig. 24 – Types of Sandals

MAKING PATTERNS - Insole and Outer Sole

1) Take a piece of cardboard, or cartolina, or drawing board or in some places called Construction Board. Place one of your feet on it and while standing firmly begin tracing the edge of that foot. It is suggested that someone do the tracing for you so that the weight of your body will contribute on the exact fitting of your sandal. NOTE: Always hold the pencil at 90 degrees angle. Do not allow the pencil lean outwards the edge of the foot tracing or inward towards the sole of the foot. Maintain the 90 degrees angle all the time.

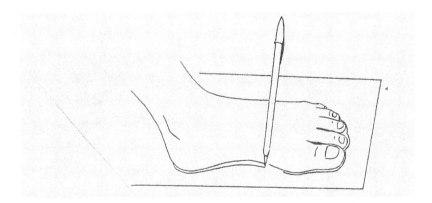

Trace your bigger foot with a pencil. It is suggested that someone do the tracing so that the full weight of your body can contribute on the exact fitting of your sandal. Always hold the pencil at 90 degrees angle.

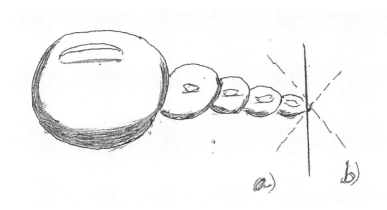

Looking at the front position of a foot, the broad continuous line represents the correct position of your pen or pencil. The dotted lines represent the wrong position of your pen or pencil.

Fig. 25 – Tracing the foot

2) Once tracing is done do not remove your foot yet. While still standing locate the highest point of the arch of that foot and mark that place on the board with a line or two. On the accompanying sketch proper markings of the different types of sandals are shown for your guidance. NOTE: Do not proceed tracing the next foot without deciding what type of sandal you want to make.

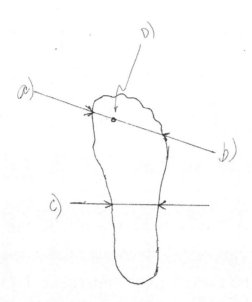

Fig. 26 – Arrows show where strap will be placed
a) in front or at the back of the big toe b) in front or at the back of the smallest toe c) at the highest point of the arch across the instep d) between the big toe and the toe next to it. (only for either Japanese sandal or thong sandal)

3) a) If you decide you want to make a Japanese sandal, mark the deepest point between the big toe of your foot and the next toe. And also where you will place the end of the 2 straps that is near the arch and heel.

b) If you decide to make a toe sandal otherwise known as Indian chappal mark the outer joint of the big toe and the highest point between the big toe and the next toe. Also, mark the insole where you will put the strap that will hold the instep.

Then mark that place where you will put the toe strap.

c) If you decide you want a 2 strap sandal, mark the front OR back of the large joint of your big toe and small toe. NOTE; since you already made the mark of the highest point of your arch extend the mark at the other side of the outline of your traced foot.

4) Once proper markings were done, remove your foot on the cardboard and mark it either right or left foot.

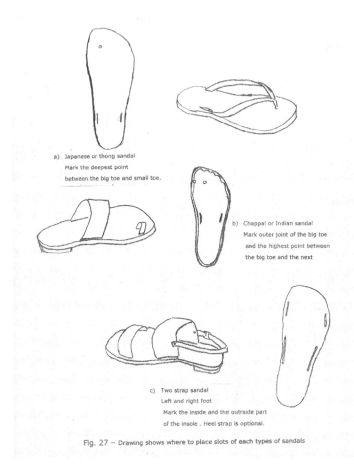

a) Japanese or thong sandal
Mark the deepest point
between the big toe and small toe.

b) Chappal or Indian sandal
Mark outer joint of the big toe
and the highest point between
the big toe and the next

c) Two strap sandal
Left and right foot
Mark the inside and the outrside part
of the insole . Heel strap is optional.

Fig. 27 – Drawing shows where to place slots of each types of sandals

5) Repeat the same procedure for your next foot.

6) Once tracing has been done both for left and right foot, make a parallel line on those outline as shown on the accompanying drawing. The parallel lines at the joint of the big toe to small toe should be 1/4 inch from the outline or footprint. From that point to the entire footprint the distance is 1/8 inch.

7) In order to avoid confusion once this pattern are transferred to the actual material, mark right away which is left foot and which is right foot

8) After all the necessary markings and the parallel lines on your footprint are done, cut the cardboard as this will be your pattern for your In-sole.

9) Insole patterns should have the markings where straps will be placed. Meantime, the outer sole will not have any markings at all.

10) Once the insole pattern has been cut, trace that pattern on a separate cardboard in order to make the outer sole pattern.

11) Before cutting the traced pattern, draw a ¼, inch parallel lines along the traced pattern as this will be your outer sole pattern. Once the parallel lines are drawn, cut the cardboard and mark surface outer sole.

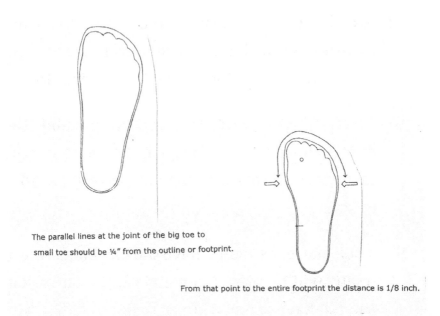

The parallel lines at the joint of the big toe to small toe should be ¼" from the outline or footprint.

From that point to the entire footprint the distance is 1/8 inch.

Fig.28 – Making the in sole pattern

12) Now you have two cut sole patterns. One for the insole, with markings where you will insert the straps, and the other sole pattern without the markings.

PATTERNS FOR STRAPS

Use a heavy brown paper or fabric (a thin canvass will do) to make specific straps you want. You can experiment with various width if you want.

Japanese Sandal

1) Make two straps, for the Japanese Sandal with a width of ¾ inch to 1 inch wide and long enough to run from the middle of the big and small toe, through the hole located near the highest part of the arch which is enough to "hold" the foot. NOTE: It is necessary that the allowance that will be "pasted" or attached or cemented under the insole is about 1 to 2 inches long.

2) Remember that after transferring this pattern on the material, one of the ends of the material will be joined together to form a thong.

Toe Sandal or Chappal

1) Make two arch straps 2 inches wide and long enough to wrap around your foot or around your instep starting from the top side of the insole seeing to it that the two ends has an allowance that can be cemented underneath to this insole. Allowance should be around 1 to 2 inches.

2) Make another ¾ inch straps to wrap around your big left and right toes. The length will be

long enough to go around this big toe. Be sure that you include the allowance that will go under the insole. Allowance to both ends that will be cemented underneath the insole is about one to two inches.

Two strap sandals

1) Make two arch straps 2 inches wide long enough to go over or "hold" the arch and instep of your feet starting from the top of the insole then make two ends have an allowance that can be cemented underneath the insole.

2) Make two toe straps 1 ¼ inches wide and long enough to go over or "hold" the big and small toes. Have the two ends have allowance that can be cemented underneath the insole. The allowance underneath the insole should be from 1 inch to 2 ½ inches for the instep strap and 1 inch to 1 ½ inches for the small 5 toes.

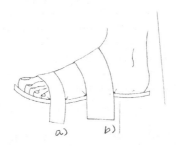

Fig. 29 – Position of the two straps
a) to hold the small and big toe b) to hold the instep

(Optional) If you wish to have an ankle or heel strap intended for the two - strap sandal follow the following procedure:

NOTE: Even without the pattern you can proceed in making a heel strap sandal. Using the same upper material;

A) Make 3 straps with a ½ inch or 5/8 inch width and long enough so that they will go around your heel and just below the ankle bone. Remember, one of the straps here will be used as a mock heel strap in order to mark where the real heel strap will be riveted. Also, the width of the strap is always dependent of the width of the buckle.

B) Make another 2 straps with the same width (½ inch to 5/8 inch) and long enough to hold the buckle. NOTE: The length of the buckle strap is approximately 1 ½ inch minus the allowance that will hold buckle or when you rivet one end of this strap to the arch strap buckle will not directly touch the ankle bone. Buckles are usually placed the ankle bone.

In order to make the ankle or heel strap straight, use a rule or steel square

TRANSERRING PATTERN OF STRAP ON THE MATERIALS

If the patterns are already on the thick cardboard, then trace it on the true side of the material using either a pencil or pen. Then cut the edges with a knife or scissors.

ASSEMBLING THE SANDAL

Japanese or thong sandal

1. Assuming you have the mark for this type of sandal (mark is between the big toe and small

toe) and the two long cuts that has the same width of the straps opposite each end of the foot, punch a round hole on the insole both the left and right feet near the toes and make the cut as shown.

2. Join the two ends of the straps that will hold the toes to make the thong. NOTE: While joining the two ends see to it that the end of the thong has an allowance that will enable the thong to be cemented under the insole.

3. Insert the thong in the punched hole. Once the thong has been inserted then spread the allowance on opposite ends and begin applying the contact cement. NOTE: Generally, make the surface of the material rough using the sandpaper before applying the contact cement. Apply the cement on both surfaces that will be joined. Contact cement meantime needs a drying time of about 5 to 10 minutes before you can join the two surfaces. Likewise, apply a very thin coat of cement on both sides to make the bonding effective.

4. It is recommended that you make it sure that the toe strap has been securely cemented before

you insert the other end of the strap. Also, you will have a good fitting if you put your foot (on standing position) onto the insole while inserting the straps.

5. If you feel that that the fitting is good enough for you then, mark the strap (the one that touches the insole) and remove your foot.

6. Follow the same procedure in inserting the straps for the other foot.

7. Once the straps for both left and right foot has been securely cemented, flip the unfinished sandal showing the end straps which is now attached to the insole and begin applying contact cement on the surface of the flipped sandal and the false side of the outer sole. "False" side of the outer sole is the one that has no design. Usually, the rubber sole has a design for traction.

8. With the outer sole now attached to the insole of the left and the right foot, you now have the sandal. Now you can sandpaper (you can also use an electric motor with a sandpaper on the shaft) the edges using the no. 2 sandpaper followed by number 1.

9. Sandal is now ready to use

NOTE:

ASSEMBLING THE TOE SANDAL AND THE TWO-STRAP SANDAL (MINUS THE HEEL STRAP) IS THE SAME AS ASSEMBLING THE JAPANESE SANDAL. THE ONLY DIFFERENCE IS THAT THE SHAPE OF THE PUNCHED HOLES ON THE INSOLE IN THIS TYPE OF SANDAL IS OBLONG OR RECTANGULAR DEPENDING SOLELY ON THE WIDTH OF THE STRAPS.

ASSEMBLING THE HEEL OR ANKLE STRAP TO THE TWO STRAP SANDAL

PROCEDURE:

1) Once you have assembled the upper parts the sandal (minus the outer sole) step on it and put the marker where you can put the rivet (place) the arch straps. NOTE: Use one of the straps as mentioned on topic PATTERNS FOR TWO STRAPS SANDALS Letter "A" where making a heel strap is mentioned.

2) Starting with your right foot, wrap around one the long straps at the heel just below the ankle bone.

3) With a pen or pencil mark the places where the long and short strap will be riveted. REMEMBER; ONE END OF THE HEEL STRAP WILL BE RIVETED AT THE OUTSIDE CURVE WHERE THE BUCKLE WILL PLACED AND THE OTHER END WILL BE RIVETED AT THE INSIDE CURVE OF THE ARCH STRAP. THIS ONE IS THE LONG HEEL STRAP. Cut this long strap to serve as a pattern.

3a) Get the short heel strap where the buckle will be placed.

4) Use the two short heel strap as mentioned earlier and put the buckle on them. Use your puncher to make a hole where the tongue of the buckle will be placed. The buckle can be put in place by using a rivet. Again, remember that to make the heel sandal comfortable, the buckle should not directly touch the ankle bone. Try several times where the other end of the strap will be placed or riveted before you permanently rivet this other end. You ask somebody to help you.

5) With a rivet, put the other end of the buckled strap at the arch strap.

6) Holding the long heel strap (without the buckle) place that one end at the previously marked place of the arch strap and rivet it.

7) Once, both the short and the long heel strap are in placed, put on again the foot on the unfinished sandal so that you can punch a hole for the tongue of the buckle.

8) Repeat procedure 2 to 7 for your left foot.

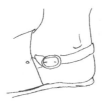

Fig. 30 – Position of the heel strap. Buckle should be placed below the ankle bone

FINISHING THE EDGES

Finishing the edges of the sandals makes the sandal much more professional looking, you can do that by using a coarse sandpaper. Get a flat narrow stick or wood around 1/2 "thick and 5" long and wrap the sandpaper on to that narrow stick. Hold a ½ inch pair of sandal against the edge of a firm surface like a table. Then, with the edge of the sandals at the edge of the firm surface, start filing the edge of the assembled sandal. Once the first 1/2 pair is done, do the same procedure on the next 1/2 pair.

Printed in the United States
By Bookmasters